MW01077719

Full Assurance

Jason R Parham

Full Assurance

A Simple Tool for Gaining Real Assurance of Salvation

2107 Gap Creek Road|Greer, SC 29651

Copyright © 2019 by Jason R Parham.
All Rights Reserved
ISBN: 9781087470023

Scripture quotations are from the King James Version.

Jason.R.Parham@gmail.com
FixerUpperMarriage.org

Cover design by Stacey Shiflett

DEDICATION

To my children- Allison, Aubrey and Jillian

You will never regret living for Jesus. I love each of you with all my heart and pray that you live a life of full assurance!

In loving memory of my precious nephew Jack, who was killed by a hit and run driver while getting the mail. His passing jolted me into publishing this book.

Why This Book?

While sitting under some of the best preaching in the world in the heart of the Bible Belt week after week, a horrifying question constantly dominated my thoughts. Every message seemed to bring my life back to the same point, that same problem, that same overwhelming question, would I go to Heaven or Hell? Satan crippled my existence with fear, torment, and confusion. Like all of my church-going peers, I made several professions as a child. Sometimes out of pressure, sometimes out of genuine fear, and even at first out of curiosity.

From Fear to Faith

As I grew older, the frustration, the sleepless nights, and the completely overwhelming fear in church set in. At seventeen, God broke my heart, and for the first time in my life, I called on God with the right motive. Obviously, burning in Hell was never a goal in my life but becoming a real Christian was not either. Needless to say, my heart changed dramatically. I returned to my public school classroom convinced I would never have another friend, to find that I had a new friend in Jesus. The seat next to me in homeroom was empty, but there was someone next to me, it was Jesus! Every morning when I awoke, I read my Bible and talked with Him. I had a real relationship with God.

From Faith to Fear

Slowly, those old fears and questions crept their way back into my life. Soon, those very fears began to torment me. Every salvation message and every effort of evangelism somehow became a source of turmoil for me. I remember the days of victory in my battle for assurance. It was wonderful to know and my spirit was lifted. However, I also remember those days of defeat, when misery and confusion plagued my thoughts.

From Fear to Hopelessness

This obviously made me dysfunctional and useless for the cause of Christ. The doubt had gripped me so deeply that no message, Bible verse, or other Christian, could say or do anything to help. Through all this struggle and torment, in my heart, I always knew I was saved, but I just could not let go of the fear. Some preachers even compounded my misery, by challenging me to question every detail of my experience, only to later tell me if had any questions about it that I couldn't really be saved. They meant well, but having never experienced my problem, they had no idea how to help.

From Hopelessness to Unrelenting Faith

God finally gave me a great victory of assurance, but not until I learned many lessons and overcame harsh personal challenges. The terrible menace of doubt had its way with me for several years, confounding my mind and blocking my spiritual growth. By God's Grace, I found my way out.

This is my story of assurance. Within the pages of this little book are remnants of battles fought and won along with Bible verses that marked my road to victory. Read carefully, and prepare your heart to learn of full assurance.

Let us draw near with a true heart in full assurance of faith, having our hearts sprinkled from an evil conscience...
Hebrews 10:22a

Table of Contents

Chapter 1

Where Are You Going?

And as it is appointed unto men once to die,
but after this the judgment:
Hebrews 9:27

Reality Check

The flames of an eternal Hell are too hot, its reality too certain, and its darkness too overwhelming to gamble with your soul. Don't take a chance on where you will spend eternity. It is the one thing in this life that you cannot afford to be unsure of. Nothing is more important than knowing where you are going when you die.

It was the greatest day of my life when I repented of my sins and put my trust in Jesus. That moment in time gave me the foundation of assurance. Without this experience of meeting Jesus, you have no recourse for finding assurance of salvation.

The Tragedy of Not Knowing Jesus

Jesus told of a rich man who lived a good, comfortable life and then died, *And in hell he lift up his eyes, being in torments,* (Luke 16:23a). Perhaps the rich man woke up one morning, going about his day. Then suddenly some terrible pain jarred his body, in his last moments he saw the room around him with a family member running to his aid. When his eyes shut, he opened them in the burning Hell. He must have been surprised to see those menacing flames, to hear the horrifying screams of millions, and to feel the worms of Hell crawling on his flesh. The rich man wasn't there because of his wealth or poverty, but because he did not know Jesus in the free pardon of sin.

How terrible to think of all the people who have opened their eyes in shock at the sights and sounds of an awful place of torment called Hell. You go about your life with rarely a thought of eternity, then death always comes when you least expect it. You live as if you will live forever on this earth, and fail to consider that you will go to the torments of Hell apart from Jesus.

God's Plan for You

You will never be good enough to avoid paying the price for your sins. The apostle Paul was a man who lived his life to the letter of the Bible, keeping even the traditions of men. Yet, he came to the following conclusion.

As it is written, There is none righteous, no, not one:

Romans 3:10

If you lived a perfect life from today on, you would still have to go to Hell for your past sins. All of your sins must be accounted for. God has made a way of salvation, but if you don't take it, you will be separated from God for all eternity. You cannot live your life neglecting His salvation and expect to live with Him in Heaven for eternity. No one is good enough to stand before a righteous and Holy God. Surely God will not send me to Hell! many would say, but in all honesty, you will send yourself to Hell by not accepting Jesus Christ.

Getting the Real Thing

When you sin, consequences follow, and payment must be made. No one has ever gotten by with sin, its consequences will find you and grip you to your destruction. When death steals your life away and your heart beats its last beat, then the payment is due. The payment is you spending a Christless eternity in Hell. There are no exceptions.

For the wages of sin is death, but the gift of God is eternal life through Jesus Christ our Lord.

Romans 6:23

The only payment that can be made is eternal separation from God. There is no checkout line for credit payments, no tabs to pay later, and no exit to run out. There is no way to run from this Creditor, no way to put it off. Death and Hell demand your life and there is no turning back once you are there.

The Good News

Jesus has already made a payment for you. However, you must accept it. Jesus suffered and shed his blood as a payment for your sins. He paid the price in full.

For when we were yet without strength, in due time Christ died for the ungodly.

Romans 5:6

It is beyond your ability to escape the payment for your sins, but God has made a provision for you through Jesus. God has no desire to send you to Hell, and He loves you enough to make a way for you to escape. The escape route is simple, but it is hard for many to accept.

You Are Just Not Good Enough

Human nature and society promote the idea that you can be good enough to earn a place in Heaven. However, the Bible teaches plainly that there is no work or goodness that will merit the favor of God.

For by grace are ye saved through faith; and that not of yourselves: it is the gift of God: Not of works, lest any man should boast.

Ephesians 2:8-9

The only favor you could ever have with God is through Jesus Christ. Moreover, the only way to have it is by accepting the payment that Jesus made for you on the Cross. He suffered at the hands of men and at a deeper level, the hands of God. He became your sin. He paid the price for your sins in full when he gave His life for you.

The Work Is Finished

There is no balance left for you to pay for your sins. What Jesus did for you is enough to give you eternal life. All you have to do is turn from your sin and ask Jesus into your heart.

It is finished were the final words of Christ on the cross. The sacrifice was complete. The method of your salvation was assured because Jesus had given His life for yours.

For he hath made him to be sin for us, who knew no sin; that we might be made the righteousness of God in him.

II Corinthians 5:21

What Can You Do?

You have to accept the payment that He has made and trust in the work that He has done for you. You must repent of the life that you have lived without Him and put your trust in Jesus Christ. No other method can reconcile you to God, no other person can forgive your sins, and no other way can get you to Heaven. Practically, it means that you ask Jesus to save you, meaning it in your heart.

That if thou shalt confess with thy mouth the Lord Jesus, and shalt believe in thine heart that God hath raised him from the dead, thou shalt be saved. For with the heart man believeth unto righteousness; and with the mouth confession is made unto salvation.

Romans 10:9-10

For whosoever shall call upon the name of the Lord shall be saved.

Romans 10:13

If you have never met Jesus, bow your head right now and ask Him for forgiveness and salvation. Just ask Him to come into your heart and save you. You don't have to live another moment without Jesus. God has given the choice to you, so chose Jesus!

The truth is that full assurance can only come from real salvation. The torment of doubt and the awful fear of Hell will follow you until you experience salvation by faith in Jesus Christ. Call on Him today, and you can have real peace and real assurance in your heart.

Chapter 2

Taking the First Step to Assurance

Let us hold fast the profession of our faith
without wavering; (for he is faithful that
promised;)
Hebrews 10:23

One night of confusion pushed me to a brother in the Lord with life experience in the subject of assurance. He encouraged me to read and study the entire book of I John. As I read, one verse, in particular, became the first step in my path to victory.

These things have I written unto you that believe on the name of the Son of God; that ye may know that ye have eternal life, and that ye may believe on the name of the Son of God.

I John 5:13

Can a Christian Doubt?

The fact that John wrote to those who believe so that they could know, proved to me that it is possible for a believer to doubt. Also, the fact that his reason for writing the book is so that believers may know, convinced me that other people have this same problem. John gives a two-fold comfort: first, that you are not alone in your struggle, and secondly that God cares about your assurance.

Let's face it, some people doubt simply because they are not saved, while others doubt because of their temperament, background, or lack of spiritual maturity. The idea that a real Christian cannot doubt his salvation is completely misguided. God gave many references in the Bible to assurance because He knew His people would need it.

The People Who Doubt

Some people never apply things they hear to themselves; they are always thinking of someone else the message could be for. The guy falling asleep on the other side of the church is the problem, or the rebellious teenagers on the back row are the ones who need preaching. They rarely make strides in their walk with God because of this. It usually takes a tragedy or major life event to get their attention. These are people who Satan can easily deceive because they just don't examine themselves.

The Problem with Doubters

Conversely, there are some people who over apply everything, taking everything that is said to heart. When a preacher admonishes the congregation to examine their experience, doubters think, A*m I lost?* or *Maybe I am not really saved.* God can do great things with people who are willing to apply the Word of God to their lives. However, such over examination can become detrimental to your Christian life if taken to the extreme.

Putting your faith in the shed blood of Jesus ends your need for salvation. However, if you let him, Satan will whisper words to make you fear and question your relationship with God. In those moments when questions and fears put their grip on your heart, you must stand firm on the promises of God. Take the Bible into your hand, read from its pages, memorize its promises and trust in its truth. Soon the doubts will dissolve under the power of God's Word.

Outside Influences

Some people who doubt may have things in their past, like a broken home, or physical/ emotional abuse that hinders them from fully trusting God. An unstable home as a child or memory of abuse can cripple a person from understanding the stability of God's promises.

These fears from the past can dominate your mind so much that it makes it hard for you to trust God. For example, if your parents fought or abused you and you could not trust them, you may have trouble trusting your heavenly Parent.

The Answer

Learn to meditate on the Word of God. When thoughts and fears from the past run through your mind, replace them with thinking about God's Word and His goodness. It is imperative that you use the Word of God to overcome your past. There is incredible power in His Word, and if you let it, it will help you. You can trust in His Word because God cannot lie and His promises have never failed.

In hope of eternal life, which God, that cannot lie, promised before the world began Titus 1:2

Spiritual Immaturity

There are some who in immaturity struggle with basic essentials to the Christian life, like trust. In my opinion, the biggest obstacle to assurance is spiritual immaturity.

Your lack of trust is probably rooted in your lack of spiritual growth. Doubters expect some great revelation of assurance or some monumental supernatural confirmation of salvation. It is like you are waiting on some kind of bombastic assurance from Heaven. All the while, those same doubters will spend very little time in God's Word or in prayer. This is the ultimate insult to God, who gave you these tools to help you be victorious.

The Unused Weapons for Assurance

The powerful Word of God can strengthen your faith and bring you to maturity in Christ. However, the Word is like a hidden weapon that is never used in a great battle. The enemy defeats you and keeps you from enjoying life, while the very weapons of victory have been hidden away somewhere and therefore useless.

Take up the sword of the Spirit, which is the word of God: (Ephesians 6:17) and use it to fight the attacks of Satan and your own doubts. Victory will come over doubt, but not without a growing use of God's Word.

Maturity Takes Time

Unfortunately, time and diligence are the only real methods for spiritual maturity. If doubt is taunting you, be brave and stand consistently on the Word and God. The reward of spiritual strength will come to you in time. It may be hard to accept that true assurance could take time, but the assurance it brings will be unshakable.

Keep living for God and grow in grace, and in the knowledge of our Lord and Saviour Jesus Christ. (II Peter 3:18a) and your faith, assurance, and confidence in God will grow also.

And we desire that every one of you do shew the same diligence to the full assurance of hope unto the end:

Hebrews 6:11

Tests of Assurance

The book of I John gives several tests of assurance and signs of real salvation. John was writing to give assurance to believers who were confused, and he gave them several simple tests to weigh their experience against. Interestingly, these tests are all in the present tense, things that should be happening now in your Christian life.

Assurance Is Now

There is no mention of the details of your profession, which is the first place many of us would go. John assumes that you had a starting point or a time when you came to know the Lord. The problem with personal assurance is not in the past, but the present. If you are saved, you will have evidence of the Holy Spirit working in your life right now.

Hell is filled with people who said and did all the right things but never had Jesus in their hearts. That is why the strongest assurances come from the evidence of the Holy Spirit working in your life. What is the Holy Spirit doing in your life right now? Has God worked in your life in the past? These questions have answers that either bring assurance or a realization that your Christianity is based on false hope.

The Tests

Do you keep His commandments?

And hereby we do know that we know him, if we keep his commandments. He that saith, I know him, and keepeth not his commandments, is a liar, and the truth is not in him. But whoso keepeth his word, in him verily is the love of God perfected: hereby know we that we are in him.

I John 2:3-5

Do you love your brother?

He that saith he is in the light, and hateth his brother, is in darkness even until now. He that loveth his brother abideth in the light, and there is none occasion of stumbling in him. But he that hateth his brother is in darkness, and walketh in darkness, and knoweth not whither he goeth, because that darkness hath blinded his eyes.

I John 2:9-11

We know that we have passed from death unto life, because we love the brethren. He that loveth not his brother abideth in death. Whosoever hateth his brother is a murderer: and ye know that no murderer hath eternal life abiding in him. Hereby perceive we the love of God, because he laid down his life for us: and we ought to lay down our lives for the brethren.

I John 3:14-16

Does God answer your prayers?

And this is the confidence that we have in him, that, if we ask any thing according to his will, he heareth us: And if we know that he hear us, whatsoever we ask, we know that we have the petitions that we desired of him. Hereby know we that we dwell in him, and he in us, because he hath given us of his Spirit.

I John 5:14-15

Take your time to study this book of the Bible. Look up the meaning of the words. Check the cross-references in the columns. Memorize and meditate on the verses that seem to help you. God will use His Word to reveal your true spiritual condition if you have an open heart and mind to Him. The first step is realizing the need and searching in God's Word to grow your confidence in Him. Take this first step today and I promise you will never regret it.

Chapter 3

Trusting Jesus

The LORD is my rock, and my fortress, and my deliverer; my God, my strength, in whom I will trust; my buckler, and the horn of my salvation, and my high tower.
Psalm 18:2

Total Trust in Jesus

Personal assurance can become like a complicated puzzle with thousands of pieces strewn around with the impossible goal of putting them all together. All the little pieces seem so hard to understand, so hard to see how they all fit together, and so hard to find the ones you need. Assurance, however, is not some complicated puzzle or confusing game from God. It is a simple victory. By focusing on the things you don't understand, you miss how simple and powerful your salvation really is. God makes all the details work. He puts everything together. He just asks you to trust in Him.

Full Trust Equals Full Assurance

Your level of assurance is in exact correlation to your level of trust. The more you trust Him, the more assurance you will have. If you put a lot of trust in Him, you will have a lot of assurance. Conversely, if you put a little bit of trust in Him, you will have a little bit of assurance. Total trust in Christ will generate total assurance of salvation. Notice that God never stipulates how much trust you must have to be saved, only that you have enough to call on Him.

For whosoever shall call upon the name of the Lord shall be saved.

Romans 10:13

Trust in Jesus is the ONLY way to full assurance. Never let men or the devil over complicate simply trusting Jesus. Take all those pieces that trouble you, and put them in the hands of the Lord. You will never get it exactly right on your own. There will always be a better salvation prayer, or a better place to get saved, or a better age. Just trust Him.

Misplaced Trust

On the other hand, a misplaced trust will undermine assurance and develop a false peace in your heart. Many Christian testimonies are based on something besides trust in Jesus Christ. Conversion cannot come without details like a time, a place, or a prayer. However, God never intended for anyone to trust in those things. Perfect peace will never fill your life when you are trying to trust in something besides Him.

An Unstable Assurance

Trusting in other things produces a measure of comfort, but only a feeble, unstable one. For instance, those who trust a prayer will someday find that they said the wrong words, or used the wrong model when they hear about another person's prayer. In confusion, many of these same people muddy the waters, even more, by correcting their initial mistake, with a new profession to base their trust on.

During all this time they miss the point- that faith has to be in Jesus. Misplaced trust creates a cycle of confusion and instability. Any person searching for real assurance must strip themselves of anything besides Jesus.

Stop Searching and Start Trusting

With our human mind, we search for something concrete to trust, something to hold onto for assurance. These things are innumerable including a time, a place, a prayer, parents, a preacher, repentance, and even faith. However, nothing can replace the peace that comes from simply trusting Jesus. Burn this thought into your mind right now, because you can go no further with God until you understand and practice it.

Chapter 4

Examining Christian Failures

Examine yourselves, whether ye be in the faith; prove your own selves. Know ye not your own selves, how that Jesus Christ is in you, except ye be reprobates?
II Corinthians 13:5

xamining yourself is something that God commands you to do. You should do so with an open mind and a vigilant heart. Looking at yourself in the mirror of God's Word and accepting what you see is something you have to practice if you expect a real assurance of faith.

An eternity of regret can be avoided by simply taking an honest look at your spiritual condition. What was the motive of your profession? Was it the prompting of the Holy Spirit, or was it someone pressuring you, or an experiment of curiosity as a child? Maybe others were doing it, and so you did too. What exactly are you trusting to get you to Heaven? Anything besides Jesus will lead you to a Christless eternity in Hell, so exam yourself.

Over Examination

In considering your salvation, and your failures as a Christian in particular, examining can be done to such an extreme that it hurts you. If you don't fully understand your carnal and spiritual natures, your failures and sins as Christian can drive you deep into guilt and further into doubt.

Many have asked, *How could I fail the Lord like that, if I am really saved?* Also, there are many professing Christians who have fallen prey to an over-examination of faith and failures.

I personally know people who have fallen into sin and disobedience, then looked to a new profession to deal with the guilt and shame. They tried to start over in their Christian life, only to find their problems multiplied.

The Struggle Is Real

The Apostle Paul explained the struggles of a real born-again Christian in the book of Romans:

For I delight in the law of God after the inward man: But I see another law in my members, warring against the law of my mind, and bringing me into captivity to the law of sin which is in my members.

Romans 7:22-23

The Old Man

When God saves you, He immediately gives you a new life in Him. However, he does not give you a new body. You are left to battle with the same wicked thoughts and temptations that come to every person alive.

The most spiritual person on earth still struggles with his old man. Even though you want to do what is right, you must do it over your sinful nature. When you do fail God, you have a responsibility to make that sinful mistake right, confess, and forsake it. One Bible verse puts it this way:

If we confess our sins, he is faithful and just to forgive us our sins, and to cleanse us from all unrighteousness.

I John 1:9

Sin and Fellowship

Sin is inevitable in the life of a Christian, but it is also inevitable that you will regret those sins and turn to your heavenly Father for forgiveness. If saved people never sinned, why would God write specifically to them about forgiveness?

Sin affects your relationship with Jesus, but not your standing with God. Calvary settled your standing with God, but your fellowship with the Lord is up to you. As a true Christian, your sin immediately breaks your fellowship with Jesus, bringing you unhappiness and discontentment. A saved person is never happy in sin, although it could bring a small amount of pleasure for a season. (see Hebrews 11:25)

Saved people in sin are miserable, which is a sign of real salvation. Someone who is lost will have no fellowship with God to become separated from. This is because the Holy Spirit does not live in their hearts to teach them the right way. Consider your life and failures, put them behind you, and learn from them, but never over examine them.

The Two Natures

The irony in all this is that this battle between your new nature and your old nature is, in fact, an assurance of your salvation. Lost people do not have a new nature that seeks after the things of God to struggle with their old nature.

Read Romans 7:14-25 closely, and you will find Paul going back and forth in his mind, not doing what he really wants (right things) and doing what he really does not want (wrong things). As we mature as Christians, we win out more in the battle with the old nature, but that very battle will remain until we see Jesus, and He gives us a new body.

Beloved, now are we the sons of God, and it doth not yet appear what we shall be: but we know that, when he shall appear, we shall be like him; for we shall see him as he is.

I John 3:2

There are people who say they are saved, but they only have the old man. They have no new man because they are spiritually dead. That death keeps them from enjoying the victories that real Christians can experience. They are lost in every sense of the word.

Who Wins?

Others are truly saved, yet struggle with their old nature, battling daily and suffering many losses because of spiritual weakness. The nature that you feed the most is the nature that will win out the most in your life. If you feed the old man more than your new man, the old man will win every time. However, if you feed the new man more than your old man, the new man will win every time.

Meditate on God's Word and talk to Him throughout your day, this is how you feed your new nature. However, if you fill your mind with things of this world like ungodly songs, movies, or thoughts, the old nature will win out. Even if you just neglect your spiritual nature by not praying or reading your Bible, you will lose every time.

When you fail God, do everything you can to make it right, then get up, shake it off and go on for God. Satan would like nothing more than to drag God's people into a cycle of confusion and doubt through their failures.

Chapter 5

Making a New Profession

Wherefore the rather, brethren, give diligence to make your calling and election sure: for if ye do these things, ye shall never fall:

II Peter 1:10

Starting Over

One of the most harmful things for a Christian in doubt to do is to make another profession. Countless Christians have taken this route only to find themselves plunged deeper into doubt and confusion. I have even known some Christians who change their personal testimony of salvation every few years or even months. They are not being dishonest, just confused about when they actually met Jesus. The changes in their testimony prove that.

This is a real shame and disgrace to the cause of Christ. If your problem is you don't know when you got saved, diligently searching the Bible and honestly searching your heart is the only way to settle it.

When Did it All Begin?

Consider your life at this time and the evidence of Salvation in your life right now. Is God doing anything for you? Can you locate specific answers to prayer in your life? Can you identify times when you know that God has done something special in your heart? Maybe God gave you a special measure of peace during a tragedy, maybe he spoke directly to your heart about Christian service, or maybe He gave you specific direction in a life-changing decision.

These are things reserved only for those who know Jesus as their personal Savior. Apart from calling you to salvation, the Holy Spirit cannot do a special work in your life if He does not know you. Now consider when these things began. When did God begin working in your life? Chances are you will find yourself at the true place of your conversion.

Has the Spirit of God Worked in Your Life?

A saved, born again person has the right and privilege of the Holy Spirit, but a lost person does not.

But ye are not in the flesh, but in the Spirit, if so be that the Spirit of God dwell in you. Now if any man have not the Spirit of Christ, he is none of his.

Romans 8:9

Another way of pinpointing your true time of salvation (for those with multiple professions) is by looking at each time objectively and sincerely. Is there a time that you cannot seem to get away from? Which time really stands out to you? Do you remember a time of change in your heart and life? Maybe you were in turmoil and God gave you peace about eternity? If you have real evidence of Salvation in your life right now, find that time that you know that God began working in your life, and hold on to it.

Let us hold fast the profession of our faith without wavering; (for he is faithful that promised;)

Hebrews 10:23

It's Up to You

Doubt and confusion can strangle a Christian so overwhelmingly that it seems the only way out is another profession. Always remember that salvation is a personal matter between you and God. Ultimately that is all that matters. This book or what anyone else believes pales in comparison to your knowing where you are going to spend eternity.

After prayerful consideration, if the need for a profession still dominates your life, then do it. Nail it down this time, and make your salvation sure, but understand that God does not take these things lightly:

For it is impossible for those who were once enlightened, and have tasted of the heavenly gift, and were made partakers of the Holy Ghost, And have tasted the good word of God, and the powers of the world to come, If they shall fall away, to renew them again unto repentance; seeing they crucify to themselves the Son of God afresh, and put him to an open shame.

Hebrews 6:4-6

The Problem with Starting Over

God calls making another profession (for a true Christian) a shame. See the Bible verses above. Whether you realize it or not, you are saying publicly that Christ's one death on the cross was not enough to save you.

You should trust what He did for you, not what you do or did! He has done everything for salvation. Make no mistake, He got every detail right for you! He is worthy of every ounce of trust that you have.

Childhood Professions

Salvation is a choice you make, a decision that turns your life around. It is a decision that defines the way you live. Yet there are many who claim salvation, who have never reached this decision point in their hearts. There has been no change, and the evidence of salvation is seriously lacking. This is contrary to what God says a real salvation experience is.

Therefore if any man be in Christ, he is a new creature: old things are passed away; behold, all things are become new.

II Corinthians 5:17

False Professions

Many people as children make a profession of faith in Jesus, only to grow up to live their lives for this world and themselves. God offers these people no assurance, and the lack of evidence of salvation is frightening. You are deceived if you trust in some meaningless prayer you prayed, that did nothing to change your life. False childhood professions are worthless in eternity. I have met people who are holding on to this. To them, it is a vague memory that obviously did nothing for them, or worse, they don't even remember it.

Overly Aggressive Child Evangelism

In my opinion, overly aggressive child evangelism has created situations where people live their lives thinking they are saved, then die and spend eternity without God.

Tell a child that he could be left behind, without his mommy and daddy, and it would be unnatural to not respond to such harsh words. What kind of child would not pray a prayer if you threatened them with Hell forever if they didn't pray?

Salvation is a decision that a child, or anyone for that matter, must make for themselves. They cannot arrive at this decision until they reach a time in their life when they have enough understanding to do so. There is no specific age, and it is dependent on the individual.

Also, it is the Spirit of God who whispers in the heart of a child the need for repentance and faith. It is important to wait and allow the Spirit to reveal himself to a child. The job of parents and Christian workers should be to teach them and gently point them to Jesus.

Follow the Evidence

A look through God's Word reveals that Biblical assurance is based on personal evidence of salvation, not a time of prayer or some profession in your past. If God really saved you, evidence will follow in your life. If there is no evidence of salvation, then you should question your salvation.

If God has not worked in your life, let go of the feeble profession you made as a child and ask Jesus into your heart. Are you willing to step out into eternity on the false profession that you made as a child? People have no evidence of salvation, yet still, point to some profession that they cannot even remember. This is dangerous and foolish. Let go of it.

Curiosity or Conviction?

Children are naturally curious, and that curiosity, mixed with a little fear, can lead them to a profession of faith. However, curiosity and fear are not the grounds for making a decision to receive Jesus as your personal Savior. I have even heard of people, who made professions as children because everyone else was. Children who make professions based on these things and grow past the age of accountability without receiving Christ will go to Hell if they do not trust Jesus.

God does not expect children who do not understand to make a decision about eternity. Moreover, He does not hold them accountable until they do understand. The plan of salvation is a simple one, but the decision is of life-long consequences and requires your exercised free will. Also, a child is not ready for salvation, if they have never experienced the conviction of God's Spirit.

It takes a lot of discernment through prayer for a parent, teacher, or ministry worker to know whether a child is ready. However, It takes little discernment to know when someone is holding on to a false childhood profession that did not give them a new nature!

The Real Thing

I personally know Christians who have real evidence of salvation who were saved at an early age. Obviously, if evidence of salvation is present, you can safely deduce that these professions are real. Salvation is a personal matter and only you can know whether you have received Christ as your Savior or not.

During Jesus' earthly ministry, children came to Him. Jesus laid his hands on their little heads and prayed. When the disciples saw this scene, they rebuked the children, but Jesus wanted them to stay. He wanted them to know who He was and that He cared about them.

Then were there brought unto him little children, that he should put his hands on them, and pray: and the disciples rebuked them. But Jesus said, Suffer little children, and forbid them not, to come unto me: for of such is the kingdom of heaven. And he laid his hands on them, and departed thence.

Matthew 19:13-15

The principle here is clear, that God cares and expects children to come to him. We can then reasonably conclude that children can receive Jesus as their personal Savior.

The Age of Understanding

Nevertheless, God expects a confessing sinner to understand what sin is and why you need forgiveness. After giving the parable of the sower, Jesus explained its meaning, illustrating this point:

When any one heareth the word of the kingdom, and understandeth it not, then cometh the wicked one, and catcheth away that which was sown in his heart. This is he which received seed by the way side.

Matthew 13:19

Obviously, Jesus does not mention age, only that there must be understanding regardless of age. The world's most serious Bible students will admit to a limited understanding of many spiritual things. However, God only expects you to understand sin, righteousness, and judgement to come when you approach Him for salvation. It is simply knowing enough to know that you need Him.

Salvation is between you and God, so forget about what others say, and take an honest look at your life. You are the one who will live with your profession of faith for all of eternity. Where is the fruit of your salvation? Where is the evidence that you know Jesus? Has God ever worked in your life?

You may have to swallow your pride in order for the truth to come out in your life. If God saved you as a child, hold onto that profession, hold on to Jesus with all your heart. However, if you made a meaningless profession, then let it go and let God take over your heart and life. Where are you going to spend eternity?

Chapter 6

The Holy Spirit's Role in Assurance

The Spirit itself beareth witness with our spirit,
that we are the children of God:
Romans 8:16

The Holy Spirit's role in conversion has become very controversial over the years. The thoughts run from a just repeat after me idea of salvation to a more Calvinistic approach of wait for deep, deep Holy Ghost conviction to fall. It is misguided to think that without regard to motive or any understanding an individual could pray a prayer that is meaningless to them and be saved. Just as misguided is the idea that you have to ask God to save you until you are sweating, shaking, and experiencing any number of extreme emotional responses before God will really save you.

What was the motive of your conversion? Was it because your friends were getting saved, or that you were in trouble, or that you felt pressured to pray? The Holy Spirit makes you sick of your sin and the things of this world, leading you to repentance. Salvation is in a person and the Holy Spirit leads you to that person, Jesus.

The Witness of The Spirit

The Holy Spirit does has a definite role in assurance. Notice the following verse:

The Spirit itself beareth witness with our spirit, that we are the children of God:

Romans 8:16

The Holy Spirit has the job of confirming your relationship with God. He will not send a postcard in the mail, or leave some kind of sign in the back yard to let you know you are really saved. However, He will, with a still small voice, confirm your position and agree with your spirit that you are a child of God. Notice the proceeding verse:

For ye have not received the spirit of bondage again to fear; but ye have received the Spirit of adoption, whereby we cry, Abba, Father.

Romans 8:15

A child loves his father and turns to him for comfort. The Holy Spirit makes that a reality with your heavenly Father. He bears witness of that Father/child relationship. Nothing in the world can replace the peace that only the Holy Spirit can give you.

You Must Be Close Enough to Hear

The Holy Spirit will speak to you, but you must be close enough to hear His voice. Drift away or covet sin in your heart, and you cannot hear that still small voice (see I Kings 19:11-13) that is the Holy Spirit. For example, if you were standing a few inches from me right now, it would probably be easy to hear me speaking. However, if you were 200 yards away from me, I would have to really raise my voice!

The witness of the Holy Spirit is the same way. His voice becomes harder to hear, the farther away you are from Him. God perfectly illustrated this in the Second Epistle of Peter.

But he that lacketh these things is blind, and cannot see afar off, and hath forgotten that he was purged from his old sins.

II Peter 1:9

How could anyone forget they are saved if the Holy Spirit is telling them that they are? The answer is, they let sin distance them from the promptings of the Spirit and could not enjoy that assurance. Trust Christ, draw close to him, and you too will enjoy that blessed assurance that comes from the sweet Holy Spirit.

Draw nigh to God, and he will draw nigh to you. Cleanse your hands, ye sinners; and purify your hearts, ye double minded.

James 4:8

Believing God

Unfortunately, your feelings fluctuate because your emotions are carnal. Some mornings I feel really saved! During these times, I just want to shout to the Lord and praise Him for His goodness. However, I have to admit that many times I just don't feel saved! This is because my feelings are liable to change. Thank God my salvation stays the same, despite the way I feel. Assurance of the Holy Spirit is not related to how you feel, but how you believe. Read the following verse with an open mind:

For the which cause I also suffer these things: nevertheless I am not ashamed: for I know whom I have believed, and am persuaded that he is able to keep that which I have committed unto him against that day.

II Timothy 1:12

Faith Before Feelings

The exercising of faith always produces assurance of salvation. Faith comes first, then comes the feelings. Basing your assurance on your feelings will spin your spiritual life into a terrible mess of confusion. Just believing Jesus and the Word of God will bring a constant assurance, even the assurance of the Holy Spirit! He alone is worthy of your trust. His power and love can comfort your heart as nothing in the world can.

How many Christians could witness the Gospel to the lost, take a stand for the Lord, or even become a preacher if only those doubts in the back of their mind would disappear?

Faith Takes Time to Grow

Unfortunately, for many of us, this full assurance does not come instantly; it takes some time for our maturity. You, however, this very day can settle in your heart that you will overcome doubt in your life. Don't give up when the battle gets intense, remember that God is bigger than any doubt you could ever face. Look at what God's Word has to say about it:

And hereby we know that we are of the truth, and shall assure our hearts before him. For if our heart condemn us, God is greater than our heart, and knoweth all things. Beloved, if our heart condemn us not, then have we confidence toward God.

I John 3:19-21

Overnight assurance could one day lead to overnight doubt, but a galvanized faith in Jesus can never be shaken. Also, if assurance came easily, then doubt could creep its way back into your heart just as easily. Give Jesus time to teach you how to lean on Him. Let Him guide you through all the fears and questions you may have. Let Him build in your heart an unshakable faith in Him.

The hardest fought battles give the sweetest victories to those who put their trust in the hands of our wonderful Redeemer! Never forget the comforting words of Scripture, God is greater than our heart, and knoweth all things. What a wonderful blessing to know that He knows my heart, my puny faith, and understands that I am only human! You may struggle with doubt throughout your life, but He has no doubts about you. He loves you and one day when you see Him face to face, He will erase every ounce of doubt from your mind.

Remember this, that no one has ever, and will ever go to Hell trusting Jesus Christ! I will write that again just in case you missed it. No one has ever, and will ever go to Hell trusting Jesus Christ.

Chapter 7

Overcoming Fear

For God hath not given us the spirit of fear; but of power, and of love, and of a sound mind.
II Timothy 1:7

The What-ifs

Doubt has its origin in the timeless question, what if. It breeds fear and uncertainty in the heart of whoever will allow it room to grow. One what if that is allowed to fester will reproduce into hundreds of them. A tiny what if can even become a terrible, looming monster in the heart and mind of the unsuspecting Christian.

What if I didn't say the right thing? What if I really didn't get saved? What if something wasn't right when I made my profession of faith in Jesus? What if I didn't understand everything? Once the what-ifs take over, the questions just keep coming. Unfortunately for many Christians, these questions are life-defining. Somehow the what-ifs always come back to bring them down. Satan loves the what-ifs, and he will not rest until they take you into confusion. The devil will give you all the what-ifs he can think of, knowing how effective they are in crippling a Christian willing to live for Jesus.

What If the What-ifs Are Real?

Are the what-ifs that keep turning up in your mind a real possibility? Yes, they are. Many people are deceived about eternity, and you could be one of them. However, it is important to remember that people who are deceived about salvation don't have evidence of the Spirit working in their lives.

Many will say to me in that day, Lord, Lord, have we not prophesied in thy name? and in thy name have cast out devils? and in thy name done many wonderful works? And then will I profess unto them, I never knew you: depart from me, ye that work iniquity.

Matthew 7:22-23

The What-if Mindset

If we all had the what-if mindset, Satan would have a heyday ruining the lives of born-again Christians. He does with many. The fear, frustration, and confusion that the what-ifs bring are absolutely devastating. The truth is, many people struggle with this problem, but embarrassment keeps them from admitting it.

Honestly, Jesus is the only real thing that is certain about your salvation. Moreover, your faith in Him is the only thing that can connect you to that certainty. It is important to understand that really the only if is knowing Jesus. It doesn't matter what questions you have or what fears loom in the back of your mind, trusting what Jesus did for you is the most important thing can do. These fears and what-ifs overcome you because your faith in Jesus is weak. The only way to strengthen your faith in Him is reading and meditating on the Word of God.

So then faith cometh by hearing, and hearing by the word of God.

Romans 10:17

Sudden Fear

Sometimes the weakness of your faith brings a sudden fear. You may be sitting in church, driving down the road, or going about your daily routines when a sudden fear enters your mind and the what-ifs overtake you.

Many people have confused sudden fear or panic for the working of the Holy Spirit. The Spirit of God convinces you of sin, righteousness, and judgement to come (John 16:8), but this is only to those who are not saved. The Holy Spirit will not try to lead someone to salvation who already knows Jesus as their Savior.

Fear or Conviction?

The Spirit will lead you to salvation in Christ and not into confusion and torment. Fear and conviction are two different things. Conviction is God dealing with your heart in an attempt to persuade you to get your heart and life right with Him. While fear is anxiety about what could be or the unknown. Conviction by the Holy Ghost can and often produces fear. However, this fear is not attached to confusion or torment. The call to salvation by the Spirit is intended to lovingly draw to Christ, not to confuse you.

For the true professing Christian with real Biblical evidence of salvation, conviction for salvation will never again come. Nevertheless, fear can come again as long as it is allowed. Fear can come unexpectedly, but it must be differentiated from God-sent conviction for salvation.

For God is not the author of confusion, but of peace, as in all churches of the saints.

I Corinthians 14:33

Be not afraid of sudden fear, neither of the desolation of the wicked, when it cometh.

Proverbs 3:25

To Know Him is to Trust Him

The solution to overcoming fear and the questions that every Christian can have is a growing relationship with Jesus. The better you know Him, the easier it is for you to trust Him! Put the what-ifs behind you, and go on for Jesus. When Satan tries to bring them back up, you bring up what Jesus did for you!

The Unknown

Another instigator of doubt for a Christian is the unknown. The unknown is foreboding and scary. We know from the Word of God that we will be in Heaven with Jesus and our loved ones (I Thessalonians 4:15-17). What we don't know, however, is exactly how this will happen, or even how it can happen. No one knows what it is like to die, so we live with the fear of what will happen, or what death will be like. This is where faith comes in. You trust Him to take care of the things you cannot see.

The Fear of Death Is Natural and Normal

God gave us all a fear of death to protect us from dying. We wear a seat belt in case our car crashes. We carefully read the labels on all our prescription medications to keep from over medicating ourselves. We look both ways before we cross the street. We go inside at the first sign of lightning. The fear of death is real and natural.

Furthermore, having a fear of dying or of the unknown does not reflect your position with God. Your position with God is unmovable, regardless of any fear you may have. If you fear, it does not necessarily mean you are lost, it could just mean that you are afraid.

The Grace and Peace to Die

In a spiritual sense, Jesus took the sting out of death. Many a martyr for Christ has walked to certain death in complete confidence knowing it was their time. Many a Christian has faced the menacing clouds of approaching death with a perfect peace from God.

O death, where is thy sting? O grave, where is thy victory?

I Corinthians 15:55

God gives you what you need for right now, and He will give you the peace that you will need tomorrow. However, He does not give you that special grace to face death, if you are not facing it! He leaves you with that natural fear of dying and of the unknown that keeps you safe and healthy.

God wants you to make preparations to meet Him and to take care of your family. However, He does not want you constantly meditating on the fear and the uncertainty of death. When death finally catches you, you will be with Jesus and have perfect peace in Him. Until then, you have to learn to live with the peace and grace that you need today and trust God for the peace and grace you will need tomorrow.

And let the peace of God rule in your hearts, to the which also ye are called in one body; and be ye thankful.

Colosians 3:1

Chapter 8

Recognizing the Enemy

*Be sober, be vigilant; because your adversary
the devil, as a roaring lion, walketh about,
seeking whom he may devour:*
I Peter 5:8

The Oldest Method

Satan's favorite weapon is fear and doubt. Make no mistake, he will use it without hesitation on the Christian who would attempt to grow in the Lord. The devil knows that nothing can be more spiritually crippling than doubt in the life of a Christian. If you are not sure about your salvation, how can you be sure about anything you do for the Lord? He began in the Garden of Eden bringing doubt on the Word of God. He manipulated what God had told Eve, convincing her to disobey God in unbelief. It only took a few minutes for Satan to destroy everything that God had been doing for Adam and Eve.

Now the serpent was more subtil than any beast of the field which the LORD God had made. And he said unto the woman, Yea, hath God said, Ye shall not eat of every tree of the garden?

Genesis 3:1

Who would have thought that a few simple seeds of doubt would lead to The Fall of Man? Second-guessing God's promises will always lead to spiritual destruction. Even though God's Word plainly reveals the promises of God, the devil will stop at nothing to make you question every one of them. The promises that God has made about salvation are plain and simple, but it is the devil who complicates and confuses them.

The Attack of Satan on the Christian

Many times, doubt is nothing more than an outright Satanic attack on the Christian trying to live for Jesus. The unsuspecting young Christian is caught off guard, and even an older Christian in the Lord can succumb to the sneaky, wicked ways of Satan. It starts with a small thought, a simple question, or a quiet suggestion. Soon it becomes a terrifying mountain of guilt and confusion. The Devil will fight with all his might to rob you of your faith in God's promises.

The Lie

Satan will try to make you think that God is angry with you, waiting and wanting to send you to Hell. On the contrary, God is love (I John 4:8), and He wants you to be saved and know it. Let's put it another way, God is for you! You just have to have simple faith in His Word. Consider that His Word will never change, It will never say anything different than what It says now.

Heaven and earth shall pass away, but my words shall not pass away.

Matthew 24:35

The Tactics

Putting your faith in what God has said is the only way you will ever have real peace and real assurance in your life. Satan will attempt to steal that faith from you by any means necessary.

He will plant thoughts in your mind, whisper half-truths in your ear, whatever it takes. He will even use Christians with good intentions to throw a cloud of doubt over the simple truths of God's Word.

As long as his tactics are working, he will keep using them. Half the battle is realizing exactly what is going on. The naive and unprepared Christian will stay in a constant state of confusion. Don't let him beat you down. When you are afraid, When you are weak in faith, let go and fall into the arms of Jesus. Just trust Him. If you allow doubt to overtake you, you will become useless for the cause of Christ. However, it does not have to be that way for a child of God. You can overcome doubt with God's help.

The Bible Answer

Submit yourselves therefore to God. Resist the devil, and he will flee from you. Draw nigh to God, and he will draw nigh to you. Cleanse your hands, ye sinners; and purify your hearts, ye double minded.

James 4:7-8

Submission is the first step that God gives you in overcoming Satan. Yielding to God will open your heart to the ministry of the Holy Spirit. Also, sin and disobedience to God are sure paths to doubt and confusion. The Holy Spirit cannot work in your life if you are resisting Him. Submit to God in your heart if you want to know what real assurance is.

How to Recognize the Spirit

The Holy Spirit's promptings can be differentiated from the devil by what each is attempting to make you do. The devil will not encourage you to live for God and do what is right. Conversely, the Holy Spirit will not prompt you to do something contrary to the Bible.

God will not tell you to make another profession after He has been working in your life as a Christian. He will not try to confuse you about what His Word says. When He speaks, it is clear in your heart. His call to repentance is unmistakable. Remember that God is not the author of confusion, but of peace (I Corinthians 14:33).

Resist the Devil

Secondly, the text above calls you to resist the devil. Don't listen to what he has to say. Reject the words and thoughts that draw you away from God and peace. When he whispers to you, it is to destroy you and render you useless for God.

Drive those thoughts of doubt away with simple Bible verses and promises from God. Don't even allow Satan to re-interpret them, remember, he is a liar and the father of it. (John 8:44). Satan is not worth listening to. The Christian submitted to God and resisting the devil can overcome his wicked intentions. This is a promise from God!

The Bible says some of the most helpful words for the Christian under Satanic oppression, and he will flee from you! God says that the devil will leave you alone if you resist him! Thank the Lord, that evil manipulator does not stand a chance against the power of the Holy Spirit and the Word of God! You don't have to doubt. You don't have to listen to the devil. You can live every day knowing you are saved and on your way to Heaven and there is absolutely nothing the devil or Hell can do to change it. Amen!

Chapter 9

Helpful Scripture Verses

...for thou hast magnified thy word above all thy name.
Psalm 138:2b

That by two immutable things, in which it was impossible for God to lie, we might have a strong consolation, who have fled for refuge to lay hold upon the hope set before us:

Hebrews 6:18

In hope of eternal life, which God, that cannot lie, promised before the world began;

Titus 1:2

For the which cause I also suffer these things: nevertheless I am not ashamed: for I know whom I have believed, and am persuaded that he is able to keep that which I have committed unto him against that day.

I Timothy 1:12

The LORD is good, a strong hold in the day of trouble; and he knoweth them that trust in him.

Nahum 1:7

The Spirit itself beareth witness with our spirit, that we are the children of God:

Romans 8:16

The LORD is my rock, and my fortress, and my deliverer; my God, my strength, in whom I will trust; my buckler, and the horn of my salvation, and my high tower.

Psalms 18:2

As far as the east is from the west, so far hath he removed our transgressions from us.

Psalm 103:12

Therefore if any man be in Christ, he is a new creature: old things are passed away; behold, all things are become new.

II Corinthians 5:17

And let the peace of God rule in your hearts, to the which also ye are called in one body; and be ye thankful.

Colosians 3:15

But if we walk in the light, as he is in the light, we have fellowship one with another, and the blood of Jesus Christ his Son cleanseth us from all sin.

I John 1:7

For if our heart condemn us, God is greater than our heart, and knoweth all things.

I John 3:20

Thou wilt keep him in perfect peace, whose mind is stayed on thee: because he trusteth in thee.

Isaiah 26:3

These things have I written unto you that believe on the name of the Son of God; that ye may know that ye have eternal life, and that ye may believe on the name of the Son of God.

I John 5:13

Thank You

Thank you for purchasing *Full Assurance: A Simple Tool for Gaining Real Assurance of Salvation*. If this book has been helpful to you in any way, consider partnering with me by doing one or all of the following three things:

Pray that God will get this book to the people who need it. This is why I wrote the book.

Tell someone else about the book. I believe the truths detailed in this book could change people's lives if they knew about it.

Share an honest review on Amazon. This helps other people searching on Amazon find the book or make a decision about purchasing it.

About the Author

JASON R PARHAM is a passionate Christian with a heart for the local church and the home. He teaches the Fixer Upper Marriage Class, writes marriage help articles, and hosts the Fixer Upper Marriage Podcast. He and his wife Amber, love serving the Lord with their three children and spending time together as a family.

Questions

1. Write down the details of your salvation experience. (When, where, etc.) This is helpful to have as a reference.

2. List the evidence of salvation in your life right now and from your past.

3. If you don't have full assurance, what are some practical steps you can take to get it?

4. Write out and memorize one Bible verse that you have found helpful about assurance.

5. What time, where, and how long are you planning on reading your Bible everyday?

6. What does the Bible ask you to do in order to be saved or become a Christian? (see page 21)

7. What are the *old* and *new* natures? (see page 42)

8. What can you do in order to hear the Holy Spirit? (see page 62)

9. Why do you think Satan does not want you to know you are saved? (see page 77)

Personal Notes

Made in the USA
Columbia, SC
03 July 2024

38032575R00057